PoEtIc

XpReSsIoNs

Volume 2

By

The Xpressions Group II

Published by

B.O.S.S. Publishing, LLC

General Information

PoEtIc XpReSsIoNs

The Xpressions Group II

All Rights Reserved. No part of this publication may be reproduced, stored in a retrieval system, or transmitted, in any form or in any means – by electronic, mechanical, photocopying, recording or otherwise – without prior written permission of the "Material Owner" or its Representative **B.O.S.S. Publishing, LLC**. Any such violation infringes upon the Creative and Intellectual Property of the Owner pursuant to International and Federal Copyright Law. Any queries pertaining to this "Collection" should be addressed to Publisher of Record.

Copyright © 2018: The Xpressions Group II

Cover Design: TP Graphics- Shantorya Jones

Publisher: B.O.S.S. Publishing, LLC

Editor: Terry L. Ware Sr.

ISBN: 978-0-9988341-2-2

1. Poetry 2. Mental Health 3. Anthology

First Edition

Credits

Organizer

Terry L. Ware Sr.

Poets

The Xpressions Group II

Book Cover Design by:

Shantorya Jones

TP Graphics

Tpgraphics15@gmail.com

Dedication

This volume of PoEtIc XpReSsIoNs is dedicated to those that have or may be dealing with any kind of depression. Know that you matter, and there is something special that is within you. May your life make a difference for those near and far.

Foreword

Depression can be a serious matter to deal with. The crippling effect it has on one's mind, body, and soul, as it is relentless with its attack, can be devastating. The dark place that it sends a person into is deeper than a grave, yet, as shallow as a puddle of water.

It is so refreshing to have a person like my dear friend, Author Terry L. Ware Sr., to combat this mentally debilitating disease by helping to bring awareness to this monster called depression. Author Terry L. Ware Sr., along with a host of very talented poets, will shed a light on this darkness with a fury unleashed with words and expressions through poetry.

Depression needs to be aware that war has been declared and this company of poetic soldiers won't stop shining bright, so that those in the deep and dark depths of depression are delivered and set free from its deadly grips. This is more than just words. This is more than just poetry. This is more than just a book. This is war! Every small victory is still a victory.

Let the words of these poets move the masses to combat the darkness with light, tears with smiles, sadness with joy. Trust me when I say this, you're not going to want to put this book down!

Author Antonio D. Thomas

Table of Contents

Dedication..iv

Foreword..v

Depression State Of Mind..........................1

    Terry L. Ware Sr

Chapter 1

Situational Depression..4

    I Will Succeed- Maggie Williams..............................5

    Starting Over- Xavi Parker.......................................7

    Soul Tormented- LaShawn Tait...............................10

    Stuck In A Moment- Carmen Floyd.........................13

    Let It Go- Isaac Crawford.......................................16

Chapter 2

Bipolar Disorder Depression.....................20

    She Is Me- LaShawn Tait……………………21

    Chemical Imbalance- Carmen Floyd……………24

    I'm Good- Isaac Crawford……………………27

    I'm Happy, I'm Sad- Maggie Williams……………30

    Routined Emotions- Xavi Parker………………32

Chapter 3

Dysthymia Depression......................37

    It's Not That Easy- Isaac Crawford……………38

    Pain- Maggie Williams……………………40

    When Was The Last Time- Xavi Parker………42

    It Starts With You- Carmen Floyd……………46

    Consumption- LaShawn Tait…………………49

Chapter 4

Postpartum Depression....................51

    Partum Me For My Confession- Carmen Floyd…52

    One Day At A Time- Isaac Crawford……………54

    A Mothers Truth- LaShawn Tait………………58

    Awaiting Beautiful Moments- Xavi Parker………62

Baby Cries- Maggie Williams……………...…..…..66

Chapter 5
Psychotic Depression……………………......67
Yearning For Excellence- Xavi Parker……...…….68
My Unknown Darkness- LaShawn Tait………....72
Am I Going Crazy- Maggie Williams……………..76
So You Think I'm Crazy- Isaac Crawford…..……..78
Silent Killer- Carmen Floyd………………..…....…82

Epilogue
Biographies………………………….....…....85
Isaac Crawford…………….....………………....86
Carmen Floyd………………………….…………88
Xavi Parker…………………………....…………..91
LaShawn Tait……………………….....…….…..93
Maggie Williams…………………….....….……..95

HELP HOTLINES…………………….……100

PoEtIc

XpReSsIoNs

Volume 2

By

The Xpressions Group II

Published by

B.O.S.S. Publishing, LLC

Depression State Of Mind

By: Terry L. Ware Sr.

Covered in fear

Not knowing if anyone is willing to hear

Sounds from within keep me quiet

Suppressed deep down

Or

So I thought

How can the quietness speak so loudly?

How can the quietness speak so loudly?

How can the quietness speak so loudly?

It blinds my words in which I desire to say

Looking around at the sounds from frowns

Thinking

No one knows my pain

No one desires to know my pain

So they just label me

Crazy

Confused

Insane

Double Personalities

So many other things that I dare not name

But if they only took the time to see

This war within that I deal with daily

Maybe they would understand

Or maybe they still wouldn't be able to see

For the lack of care within their own selves

Covered in fear

Not knowing if anyone is willing to hear

Sounds from within keep me quiet

Suppressed deep down

Or

So I thought

Feelings that keep penetrating my brain

Uncontrollable actions seeking help not condemnation

I never pictured this being me

How can one be blinded by what they see?

Tell me

Where do I go

What can I do

Who will be the help that I so desperately need

Chapter 1:

Situational Depression

I Will Succeed

By: Maggie Williams

Coping

Hoping

Wondering is it going to end

My joy

My victory

This battle I will win

Never going to make it

Never will I succeed

Crying inside

Hiding my pride

River flowing heart with tears that bleed

Praying

Praying

Are prayers going to get answered?

Maybe one day my success will get pampered

Starting Over

By: Xavi Parker

Because of the absence of you

Eating had become extinct

Laughter inhibited a distant cry

Smiling weighed a heavy frown

What day?

What day did your presence cease to exist?

What day was my heart pulled from my chest and forced to beat a different rhythm

When you were the one who shared my heart beat for 9 months

But yours no longer had a beat

No longer had a rhythm

Your lungs no longer filled with air

Your mind no longer fed me your thoughts and compliments of my beauty

You gave me life

Only to darken the day you lost the fight for yours

The day I felt more selfish than ever

The day I wanted my life to end so hers could begin again

I sunk

Into a place of darkness

Where anything that sustained life

Was not useful in my life

I did not recognize my face

I wanted to continue to be beautiful for her

But I couldn't even begin to understand my identity without her with me

I was the sunken place

I personified the words dark and hurt

Energy only came when there was a need to cover what I felt

To please others and make them see my strength

But my outer shell was as strong as a fresh egg

Waiting to be dropped

I didn't want others to know that I was sad

Lost

Sunk

A life ended and now I had to adjust and begin my life all over again

Soul Tormented

By: LaShawn Tait

Looking into the eyes of a lost soul…

Nothing more captivating

The pains

The hurt

The emotional abuse…

All devastating

Memories of neglect in my younger years…

Camouflaged and hidden by uncried tears…

A sense of unbirthed love all tangled and thorned…

Leaves a heart of snares that beat to no drum…

But it yearns to be captured

But it strives to be free…

Mirrored images of desperation and all I visualize is me…

Hanging from a cliff

No one to catch me if I fall…

Longing for inner peace

Soul building constant walls…

Impenetrable and constantly growing

Soul has no glow…

Living a life of hidden lies all that no one should know…

Depression creeps in like a thief in the night…

Stealing my dreams cutting my throat…

Taking my life

Soul tormented by the desire to be loved…

Heart running from his presence taking flight like a dove…

The presence of a soul is now slim to none…

Realization of the ending…

When it's over it's just done…

Stuck In A Moment

By: Carmen Floyd

Again it's the end of the rope

And this moment is void of hope

No sign of my faith

What more must I take

At the moment

It's hard to cope

Before this moment there was no pain

But now all I feel is shame

Tossed to and fro about

A sudden flood of fear and doubt

So at the moment freedom is tamed

And tho I wish

I cannot share

Curse this moment

Cause I don't care

To be around anyone

Or have any kind of fun

See at the moment I'm unaware

Of how I affect anyone else

I just need a moment to myself

A moment to gather my thoughts

No matter what it cost

Can't you see that I need help

But to speak is such a task

And I'm too afraid to ask

So the fear I hide behind

Keeps me stuck in a moment of time

And the smile you see is just a mask

Yet I know this too shall pass

Sometimes slow

Sometimes fast

I'll be back in a minute

Once the moment has finished

For these moments never last

Let It Go

By: Isaac Crawford

It is so easy for someone on the outside looking in

to say

Let It Go

A simple phrase that crosses the lives of many

In a seemingly quick attempt to pacify my feelings

How can one just let it go?

You don't understand my pain

The sacrifices that I have made

You didn't see the effort that I put in

Or the feeling of joy when times were good

You have not truly walked in my shoes

To begin to break down the

How's

When's

Whys

So you just want me to simply

Let It Go?

Let go of the memories?

Let go of the feelings?

Let go of everything that was built?

Don't you realize that these things took time?

I mean I can't just let what I've known for so long go like that…

I would be so lost

I wouldn't know what to do

I wouldn't know how to move on if I just

Let It Go

But you know as painful as it may seem and as difficult as it may be to

Let It Go

That's maybe just what I need to do

Maybe letting it go won't be so bad if I did it gradually

Letting go while allowing my heart to heal and allowing my mind to release what I have been holding onto for so long

If I begin to let go

I am sure that the space that is currently being occupied by this pain and disappointment

Would begin to make room for happiness and joy

Love and fulfillment

I know that this must take place for me to move forward

I must let go so that this situation doesn't hold me back

I must let go so that I can begin the healing process

Yes it may take time and my time frame will be different from yours

But letting go I must

But let me tell you this

What I will not let go of is the lessons that I have learned while going through this process

I will not let go of the way that I felt then and the way that I feel now

So I shall begin to

Let It Go

So that I can make room for what I should be holding on to

Chapter 2:

Bipolar Disorder Depression

She Is Me

By: LaShawn Tait

My moods are up and down…

Yet I have no understanding

Thought process on a zillion…

My life is so demanding

Trying to cope with life…

Yet I'm contemplating my demise

Smiling on the outside…

But my soul constantly cries

Today I'm me…

Or maybe she's me

Or maybe together

But separate there's no we

I cannot exist without my inner me

No more than she can exist without what will always be

US

You see society would say that I'm probably bipolar...

That I'm unable to exist

That I'm not the controller...

Of my life or my thoughts

But this can't be true

Yet I foresee my future and it consists of bright areas

But mostly deep dark hues

Conflicting but it's not hard to understand...

What's known to me shall remain hidden to man

She lies hidden and dormant

But yet she still lives free

Free but yet still captive...

She is me

And with no we…

There is no she

Chemical Imbalance

By: Carmen Floyd

You're missing and it's too much to handle

I don't know what I really need

It's quiet now

It's so loud

And I'm bothered

All I want is peace

I had you

Now you're long gone

And I know it's me who made you leave

You kept trying but I frightened you

With my insanity

My mental madness is a chemical imbalance

I'm screwed up in every way but two

That's who I am and how I feel for you

And these mixed reactions from my chemical imbalance

Send me High and low and I have no control

Please don't go

I want you

But I change quick

I'll admit sometimes you make me sick

I'm lonely

Please come hold me

Get away!

I'm tired of your mess!

I hate you!

But I love you…

And the truth is who I hate is me

Cause I go up and down and round and round

I have no gravity

God

What is wrong with me

All I need is some stability

Help me!

Please make it go away

(I'm Good

By: Isaac Crawford

A feeling that won't go away…

Well it does

Then it returns

A feeling that I can't explain…

Well I can but who will learn

My thoughts are here and my emotions are there

Racing ponders of my reality

Wondering who really cares

It's not something that I can truly control

But I try my best to just cope

Relate

To not frustrate

To just let it go

But I can't

I want to

But I don't know how

I can talk about it and that seems to help

But it is so hard when I feel alone

By myself

So I'll continue to push myself forward and remember that

I can get pass this phase

If even for a moment or a couple of days

I'm good

That's what I have to tell myself

But the most important part…

Is that

I must

Believe it)

I'm Happy, I'm Sad

By: Maggie Williams

I'm feeling all alone inside

Around people my feelings I try to hide

I'm dying from pain I hold

I'm crying behind walls because my heart is getting cold

But oh no with people I'm so happy to be around

Because happiness is finally what I found

And in my mind

I'm thinking of the joy I feel

But goes back to feeling this is not real

Am I crazy

Am I lost

Am I losing my mind

For a second while thinking I thought I was fine

I am fine

I am happy

My feelings are under control

Wait

I'm tripping as I'm sipping

These crazy feelings inside

I try to hold

No I'm sure of this feeling

My thinking is so real

I'm feeling down all the time

Because my pride

Makes it hard to swallow this pill

Routined Emotions

By: Xavi Parker

Amazing!

Pure bliss!

I feel like I can conquer the world!

I want to go on a high-speed test drive!

Give a Bugatti

Hennessy Venom

Or Lamborghini a whirl

Have to feel the power behind the wheel

The same power I feel

My power is stronger than any Avenger

I am on top of the World!

I want to go

It's time to travel

Sell the house

Car

And everything else

I can leave this life behind and travel the world

See how beautiful it is

It feels so good to feel alive

I feel alive

I can feel my blood rushing

I am a super hero

I'm talking too fast?

My language is rushed?

You just can't feel my excitement is all!

My thrill!!!

I'm alive!!!

24 hours in a day and I will not waste one

This energy passing through my body is electric

Man

I wish you could feel it

I'm wired!

I'm pumped!

Let's live this life

I can live just like this for days

Weeks

Maybe even a month

But I don't want to live

I'm worried about what I will do now

Why am I here

No one even likes me

I

I simply wonder

Will people miss me

Or am I important

They will be better off without me because of my changes

I cannot remember when I enjoyed life

It's nothing but strife now

A drag

I want to remember being happy but I cannot

Maybe I should lie down

Nights are the best

I rest all day and better at night

Getting out of the bed for work is a struggle

I don't enjoy anything

Food helps me fill a void

I know I'm not like this all the time

I know this cannot be me

It'll change

Again

Give it time

This

All of this is routine to me

Chapter 3:

Dysthymia Depression

It's Not That Easy

By: Isaac Crawford

A constant struggle to push myself to keep going…

Some may say for me to just do it or it isn't that bad

But how would they know?

I'm in a consistent state of feeling

Like I have nowhere to turn

I try to talk about it

But that only pacifies the moment

Not the cause

How did I get here?

Can this feeling be reversed?

Erased

Minimized

What else can I do to ease this?

I am not sure

But I can't quit or give up

I keep telling myself that it will get better

And that thought alone helps

For I know that one day

I will feel & be better than I am today

Will that day come tomorrow?

I truly hope so

"Pain"

By: Maggie Williams

I try so hard to deal with this pain

But thoughts of it is driving me insane

Losing you makes it hard to breath

But I try hard and still seem to seethe

If I could give one last breath to have you here

Lord knows I would

To smell your scent near

Having dreams of you makes my life complete

All the laughs and fun times I could have again

I wouldn't skip a beat

Day after day I sob in my own rain

Until we meet again

Teach me angel

How to cope with this thing called

"PAIN"

"When Was The Last Time"

By: Xavi Parker

Sleep doesn't come this time

When daylight peaks

I close my curtains

And hope then that I can find sleep

But my eyes are open

And all I see is white walls

Then the question comes

When was the last time?

Memory roll call

You know

Trying to remember happy memories and all

Been a couple of years

But I try

And the memories are buried so deep

It never comes to me

Pictures of me seeming happy

But even then

I know it's just a mask

Behind closed doors

My mind begins to ponder

And conclude that happiness does not last

So I'm stuck for now

Realizing to others life is a blast

Consistently for them

To me

I'm praying I can make it through the day

Forcing a smile

I've lost interest in what excites me

Patterns of sleep are inconsistent

I hear people talking to me

But I cannot concentrate on what they are saying

I'm hopeless

Just about worthless

Recognizing everyone else happiness again

They've been happy awhile

And I continue wondering

How

How are you smiling right now?

How are you laughing?

How did you fall asleep?

How do you have joy?

How are you not fatigue?

Sometimes things are alright

But most times they're not

I'll talk it out

And for now

I will sit in the low my mind has brought me to

Self to self

When will I experience that high again

Well

For now

Only heaven knows

It Starts With You

By: Carmen Floyd

You can make a decision today and everyday

That your life doesn't have to be this way

You don't have to be depressed the rest of your life

Choose to walk into the sun

Stop avoiding the light

You can be a happy person

You can be free

You can be everything God created you to be

Instead of being silent

Lift your voice and speak

You were not born a coward

You don't have to be weak

Put yourself around the crowd

You don't have to be alone

Get out and live your life

You don't have to stay home

Your personality is a gift that was meant to be shared

Fear is only an illusion

You don't have to be scared

Everyday doesn't have to be full of clouds

You could bring the sun back

If you would only smile

Even if you have to

Force it

Fight for yourself

Cause your happiness won't come

From anyone else

If you have to

Take your meds

Don't reject the help

Every journey to better

Health starts with one step

Make it in the right direction

Don't lose your sanity

I'm not just talking to you

I had to tell this to me

Consumption

By: LaShawn Tait

My spirit is real weak...

At an all-time low

Emotional noose around my neck...

Yet it's tied like a pretty red bow

When you see my face all you see is what I allow you to see

None of the pain

That's constantly devouring me

I'm at my lowest low...

And I swear I can't get any lower

Trying to run fast to escape

But my pace has gotten slower

So I sink deeper and deeper

Into this depressing desolate state

Friends and family always ghost proving

They're fake or just maybe forsaken

So reality is

I have no one to ever lift me up

To show me real love when I'm stuck

In my own self-destruct...

So I've submerged into the deepest place of any man's existence

And I drown over and over again because of you...

***Consumption*...**

Chapter 4:

Postpartum Depression

Partum Me For My Confession

By: Carmen Floyd

I can't blame them

It's not their fault

That's what I keep telling myself

The price of kids has come at such a cost

I can't return and put back on the shelf

So depression was the battle that I fought

While I struggled with the cards I was dealt

Assuming all my dreams would come to a halt

Regretting that my virtue wasn't fully kept

Be a Queen was what I was always taught

If he's a pawn he should always be left

Now It seems that I have taken such a loss

Sometimes I'm so disappointed with myself

To nurture sometimes brings about exhaust

The stress of motherhood affecting my health

Because my heart was cold and placed in such a vault

That only God's hands could warm the ice and melt

So prayer and therapy was what I sought

And before our Father God is where I knelt

And I asked that he would pay for what I bought

For all that I had brought upon myself

One Day At A Time

By: Isaac Crawford

Overjoyed from the moment that we found out about you

Preparing for your arrival

We bought clothes and toys

Trying to wrap our minds around you

Our new arrival and the joy

Days and weeks pass

Now we are looking at months

I can feel you growing inside of me

Even more now we are one

I feel your every movement and I know when you are resting

My heart is overwhelmed

You are a blessing

It's getting closer to the day

My body is adjusting because clearly

You are on your way

Pain

Rushing

Calling ahead

Everyone is anxious to see you

We tough it out and one is now two

You are here

I feel no joy

I'm sad and I don't know what to do

I don't feel like holding you

Or caring for myself

I'm lost and I really need some help

My mind is frozen & I'm stuck in a daze

I feel like I'm trapped and my mind is a maze

I see you and I start to cry

I'm not sure if I can do this

I'm not sure if I'm ready

And I don't know why

I pray about it and the counselor is attempting to assist

I want to love my baby and take care of myself

I don't want to feel like this

It's been weeks and I want this feeling to stop

One day at a time they say

I'm attempting to get up and move around

I've got the courage to hold you now

Your smile and scent seem to help bring me out

Know I can do this without fear and doubt

That's what I'll do

One day at a time...

One day at a time

A Mother's Truth

By: LaShawn Tait

8 1/2 months I carried him growing & kicking in my womb

With his birth came my death

My demise

My heart buried deep within a tomb

My body was ripped from one end to the other

Had no desire at all

Of being this child's mother

When he came into this world

All I heard was his cry

My heart hurt

My body was sore

And all I wanted to do was just die

Never touched or comforted him

Never wanted to be a mother

Suppose to be the beginning of life but all I felt was smothered

Where was the beauty and bliss of giving birth to a first-born son

My life is now over with

With his birth he became my smoking gun

Took my life away the day that he breathed in air...

Lil beautiful brown eyes staring up at me

He wasn't even aware

Depression took over me and I despised this child for no reason at all

I wanted to run

Instead I cried

And screamed

But there was no one I could call

Subliminal messages from loved ones

Of what a mother should be

Shaking my head in disgust

While this little being looks up at me...

He's crying to be fed and I'm crying for release

From being this child's mother

All I wanted was my inner peace

I cry and I cry and so does he...

And then I finally look at his little beautiful face and all I see

Is a Lil mini me

So I closed my eyes and I asked God to please put my mind at ease

You see my Lil Chocolate Chip

He's as handsome as handsome can be

It was at that moment I finally started to love me...

Now all the love in my heart is given to my son...

At the end of the day he gave me my life

Never again from his love will I run...

Awaiting Beautiful Moments

By: Xavi Parker

Those 9 months were marvelous

Overflowing with joy

Questions of whether or not it's a girl a boy

The excitement

The wonder

Soon to become someone's mother

Giving life it is beautiful

Your birthday comes

My body changes and adjust to some of the most excruciating pain

But you are worth it

Your first cry and I stare at you

Knowing you are a jewel

But a feeling comes

Unfamiliar

Unexpected

A quick drop in hormones and the joy is gone

I regret ever getting pregnant

Never been a parent so now I want to perfect it

Goodness

I don't know if I'll ever be able to leave your side and if I do I will feel a level of guilt

As if I don't want to love you because

You're from me

I need an emotional lift

Because now there is a level of resentment

I care about you

You're me

You're my baby

I carried you

And I look at you and anxiety controls me and I cannot care for you

Only about you

I'm tired

Worried

How will I ever enjoy a night out with friends

Without worrying about your diaper needing to be changed

Over parenting and things

I'm not cut out for this

You deserve better than me

You need another mother

Crying is the only thing that's constant in my life

And I don't know why I'm crying

I push away your Uncles

Aunties

And other parts of the family

No one knows how I feel and no one can help me

I try to concentrate on silence

But thoughts continue to pile

But it's only for a little while

Then it happens

I realize my only peace is when I hold you to me

I let your breathing match my heartbeat

And we become one

A Mother's love is so deep

My baby

My peace

I feel what I feel for a bit

But in the end

When it's done

When my body and emotions began to function

I'll be happy that We

Will be sharing beautiful moments

Baby Cries

By: Maggie Williams

Babies cries is all I hear

Sounds coming loud and clear

Hurting inside wondering why

Thoughts in mind this infant should die

Truly I love you but my mind is in a daze

Banging my head and walking in a maze

Make it stop

Please smother this thing

Grabbing a pillow that someone brings

I've got to stop thinking of hurting my baby

But these baby cries are driving me crazy

Chapter 5:

Psychotic Depression

Yearning For Silence

By: Xavi Parker

I have watched the same movie

Over and over again

Not because I have a favorite line or scene

But because I cannot concentrate enough for a movie

Without my inner thoughts interrupting me

Trying to recognize any character with similar pain as mine in their eyes

Knowing it's all fiction

But I'm fixated on searching to find out

If someone feels where I am coming from

Or if it is just me

And this inner voice

Inner thoughts

Wishing I could serve them an eviction notice

But that would be homicide-suicide

I wish I could unsee some things

Even better if I could not hear anything

But It's the sound of my own voice

All this noise

Forcing me to realize my worth

The worth I do not have

I failed myself by not understanding my value

Which being worthless seems to have made me hopeless

It's obvious

I don't want life and it's not that I don't appreciate it

But I hear myself saying

"No one will miss you anyways"

"It's not like you help by being alive"

But the fact is

I cannot make the decision as to whether I should stay or leave

Sometimes I find that the old me had a sense of humor

How can I get back there?

Nothing is enjoyable

My bed has become my coffin

And tears are my morning coffee

I can't remember when I ate and when I do eat

It's always too much or too less

When will I ever be back at my best

Instead of being constantly stuck in my mental mess

You're nothing

You walk around with your head down

Introverted

Solitude

Alone

No friends

No one cares

No one can see you

Invisible

WHY DON'T YOU SHUT UP!!!

BE QUIET!

I don't want to hear how worthless I am

And how valuable I will never be

I don't need others sympathy

It wouldn't matter because the inner me has conditioned me to believe

Everything that's not even true about me

So my screams for help are silent

But I want help

I need help

I am yearning for silence because my life has become the personification of noise

My Unknown Darkness

By: LaShawn Tait

My world revolves constantly from grey and white to black real fast...

Mind in infinite places how long will this feeling last?

This blackness surrounds me always encompassing my soul...

A soul that once had a small glimmer of hope

Is now one that has been sold to the highest bidder

You can call him the Unknown...

He twists and turns my perceptions of life always leaving my heart cold

I see demons and devils every time I look into your eyes...

Constantly whispering seductive words in my ears that are nothing more than lies

Every step that I take I see you creeping up behind me...

Disguising yourself to be innocent but that's not at all what I see

My visions are in 3D and I see the real you...

Face all distorted and disfigured now that is your real truth

You're out to destroy me...

Even take my life...

While confessing your undying love and stabbing me at the same time with your knife

When I tell you I see you for who you truly are...

You call me delusional and say I keep my head up in the stars

My multidimensional thinking could never be explained...

Instead of protecting my sanity you would rather drive me insane

Calling me paranoid and psychotic and even deranged...

Yet you don't know in another lifetime I too once had your name

You see I'm the Unknown who once existed to cause you pain...

I was the one who consumed your thought process and crawled down your membrane

Wrapped myself around your cerebral cortex...

Do you now remember my name…

I was that that dark being who existed to drive you insane

Now I'm the new me and you are who I use to be...

I keep closing my eyes but in reality

You still follow me.

Please just go away

I just wanna live my life in peace...

How do I escape from your grasp when I know there will never be a release

I see now that my pain and delusional state brings you extreme pleasure....

My life my love has become nothing more than your buried treasure

Is this my fate for who I was in my past...

Again I ask you how long will this darkness last?

FOREVER

You say with a wicked smile...

You will always belong to me...

Am I Going Crazy

By: Maggie Williams

Am I going crazy

Am I losing my mind

Thinking of voices I hear from time to time

Screaming out loud

Leave me alone

Others run to the rescue to see what's wrong

Dying inside from painful thoughts

Trying to kill myself with this metal wrought

Seeing people that aren't really there

Scaring myself when the visions are rare

Yes

I'm going crazy

Being drove insane

But the voices are speaking

As my crazy thoughts begin to gain

So You Think I'm Crazy

By: Isaac Crawford

When you hear the word crazy

It's deeper than just acting weird or strange

I'm not crazy

I am not weird

I am not strange

I am however dealing with a lot

I need assistance with realizing that I will be ok

My mind doesn't work like yours so I need help

I need help from those who understand what I am going through and who truly wants to help me

I may not be able to respond the way that you believe I should

But believe me I am trying

I am really trying

But it seems to not work for me

Just when I think I am feeling better

My mind does its own thing and I begin to lose my grasp with reality

I begin to see and feel things that are not really there

Those around me that don't understand this will think that I am going crazy

But those that are familiar will know what to do and help me

That's all I really need

I need people who are willing to help me and not make fun of me

I don't want this

I didn't sign up to feel this way

It just happened

Is it my fault that I am going through this?

Honestly

I don't know

Trees are green and brown

The sky cries and we get wet

The walls can talk

I can't breathe when they do

When you hear the word crazy

It's deeper than just acting weird or strange

I'm not crazy

I am not weird

I am not strange

I am however dealing with a lot

I need assistance with realizing that I will be ok

My mind doesn't work like yours so I need help

The voices in my head are too loud

They are trying to take me away

Please don't let them

Do you live in a bee hive?

Day is night and night is day

Why don't you believe me?

When you hear the word crazy

It's deeper than just acting weird or strange

I'm not crazy

I am not weird

I am not strange

I am however dealing with a lot

I need assistance with realizing that I will be ok

My mind doesn't work like yours

So I need help

Silent Killer

By: Carmen Floyd

No one hears how it haunts

Or its repetitious taunts

No content for what I'm given

Questioning every decision

Wasting time

Time

Time

In the corners of my mind

And this torment that's been brought

Amplifies every negative thought

Curse my ear

For it's an audible to supernatural fear

Someone close the door and lock

Make it stop

Make it stop

And it hides so very well

Behind a truth that I can't tell

So they don't know

Of this voluminous silent killer

The psycho

No one sees it in disguise

How it faces me and lies

About everything that's good

And I feel so misunderstood

Forced to fake

Fake

Fake

How much more must I take

Dare I chance another look

At this imaginary crook

Curse my eye

For any hope that it beholds it surely dies

Gouge them out so I can't see

Set me free

Let me be

Cause it hides so very well

Behind a truth that I can't tell

So they don't know

About this invisible silent killer

The psycho

Epilogue

About The Poets

Isaac Crawford is a writer, poet, and entrepreneur who loves to express his creativity in everything that he does. His extensive background in the counseling/social service field has allowed him to look into people and situations with an objective yet optimistic view.

Through his life experiences and being raised in a strong Christian faith household, he understands that life is life, and we all have one to do our very best so that when it is all said and done, our "dash" speaks for itself.

"Everyone has a story, remember that you are not the author."
Isaac Crawford

Carmen (Dani Abstract) Floyd is a spoken-word artist and singer/songwriter from Montgomery, Alabama. Her childhood was full of instability and hardships that caused her to move around from one place to the next, but the one thing that remained constant in her life was her love for music and writing.

In school she always participated in whatever choral music or creative writing programs they offered and stood out amongst her peers as an exceptional writer. While attending Alabama State University her English professor was so impressed after hearing Carmen recite an essay that she presented Carmen with one of her favorite anthologies and wrote on the inside of it that she believed one day Carmen's writings would be featured in such literary works as that one. But at that time Carmen had aspirations of being a rapper. She performed under the name, Baby Doll. Soon after she decided that that wasn't the life she wanted.

Still, her love for music and writing needed an outlet so she moved to Atlanta and began writing poetry. When she returned to Montgomery she hit the stage again, but this time as a spoken word artist under a new alias, Dani Abstract, and quickly became one of her cities most notable performers. Her passion for community service lead her to become a poetic activist for such organizations as Project Hope (Aids Awareness), Crest Foundation (Substance

Abuse and AAA), attorney Bryan Stephenson's More Than Campaign (Equal Justice Initiative) and Michelle Browder's I AM MORE (Children's Outreach) to name a few.

She's also written songs for several artist and landed a position as the musical director for established playwright and film director Jona Hall's play The Other Side of The Down Low. Dani Abstract is currently a songwriter for TA1 Music Group, a contributing writer to Hype Inc. and a member of the Sole Collective. She is also the author of the poetry book, The Evolution of Carmoney. Her ambitions are to go as far as her talents will take her.

"Your peace of mind is priceless! Protect it with your life! You can't afford not to…"

Carmen (Dani Abstract) Floyd

Xavi Alexandra Jenee Parker was born on September 19, 1990, in Birmingham, Alabama. She was raised by her mother and grandmother in Clanton, AL. She has four older brothers and 2 younger sisters. She graduated from Auburn University in Montgomery, AL with her B.S. in Psychology. She started writing poems and short stories around the age of eight. Her writings were always inspirational, encouraging, and uplifting.

She continued to write throughout different stages in her life.

Xavi's biggest tragedy in life happened when she lost her mother at the age of 15. She started writing deeper pieces about society, death, life, love, etc. Some would say she was a poet, however, she does not label herself as a poet. Instead, she would tell you that she's just an artist who uses her words to paint her way through life.

"If we learn to share more of our internal scars, we could help others realize just how beautiful they really are."

Xavi Parker

LaShawn Tait is a native of a little small town in Alabama by the name of Evergreen. She is the mother of two amazing children, Mykel & TiChina and she loves her family beyond life. LaShawn started writing poetry at an early age as a means to escape her reality.

To say that she has been through a lot is definitely an understatement. LaShawn believes that God has allowed everything that happened to bring her to this point in life. None of this broke her down nor did she fold under pressure, it did however, create a beautiful Diamond that will never be absent of flaws yet is perfectly priceless.

LaShawn would always question her purpose on this earth and believes that all the time God was preparing her for this moment in time and now the Phoenix within her flows like a free spirit. What was once surrounded by darkness is now nonexistent and she is now totally encompassed by light.

"Always grow through your darkness and then you will transcend beyond this life within your own personal light."

LaShawn Tait

Maggie Williams is a proud mother of 4. She loves to read and write, as well as cook. She loves helping others and enjoys writing poems that inspire people. Maggie has been writing poems since she was 12 years old. She loves God and puts him first before everything that she does.

Maggie hopes that everyone who reads this book will be inspired by all of the poetry and hopes that God gets the glory from it.

"My life may not be going as I planned it, but it's going exactly the way GOD planned it."

Maggie Williams

GET IMMEDIATE HELP

Emergency Medical Services

911

National Suicide Prevention Lifeline

1-800-273-8255

Veterans Crisis Line

1-800-273-8255 PRESS 1

Substance Abuse and Mental Health Services Administration (SAMHSA)

1-877-726-4727

24/7 Depression Hotline

1-855-544-1070

www.ingramcontent.com/pod-product-compliance
Lightning Source LLC
Chambersburg PA
CBHW042313150426
43200CB00001B/6